Mortar

Also by Christopher Shipman:

Human-Carrying Flight Technology
The Movie My Murderer Makes
A Ship on the Line (with Vincent Cellucci)
Cat Poems: Wompus Tales and a Play of Despair
T. Rex Parade (with Brett Evans)
The Movie My Murderer Makes: Season II
Keats is Not the Problem (with Brett Evans)
Getting Away with Everything (with Vincent Cellucci)

Mortar

poems

Christopher Shipman

Brick Road Poetry Press—Birmingham, AL

for my family

Contents

Contents

I had a dream last night that I met a woman made of bricks. She took herself apart, brick by brick, and became a pile of bricks.

—Brandon Shimoda

In order to understand it, we must hear it told in many different voices, or not at all.

—Brooke Champagne

Prologue

When I miss a call from my father,
I imagine him standing
in the palm of a river. An arcane sadness
sandbagged behind the years
that followed him there.

And there—white sky—he sees a window
grow wild on the horizon.
Then another and another and again.

Glass hanging in wooden frames held up
by nothing. Any ghost invited
to enter or exit the absence of walls.

This happens every time. And every time
it's my fault—everything
that drags the riverbed snared in one net.

The poverty of an old cul-de-sac snagged
on drunken fists. Six siblings.
His mother's murder. His decision
to leave when I was born—six years gone,
winter was for forgetting.

I listen to his usual voicemail. I remember
to rise above this—to try to—
like a dream that teaches you how to fly.

I had that dream often after my father
came back. Forget the rules
for a second, you're sure to fall. Don't fly

any higher than the telephone poles. Now
try the trees. The branches
stretched over enough river to save you.

Stay safe. The voicemail repeats. *Stay safe.*
The same simple imperative
my brother gets with every missed call.
My brother—who climbs
cell towers for a living—who all day sighs

like death. Looking down from 200 ft.
I wonder what he imagines. If he swears
he's seen a mystic sadness—

its massive wings shadow over the shapes
of the city below, as if twin rivers
flowed above it. If in dreams

he follows our father with feathery arms.
Listening for his name.
Waiting to be called into the sky.

I think I should get me a dog. I'm tired of being my own dog.

—my father

I have flowers in my eyes.

—my daughter

brick

a block of dried clay

(hidden inside—
like anything else—

a museum of moments:

here the touch
of human hands

there

the heat
hands awaken)

Little Rock, AR. 1970. Larry, 27, bricklayer, imagines absence. A dark that harbors something. It waits. He can tell. Something bright against the black will blur into view. Something will glow. Take shape. There—an uncanny hand. A fist opening. He can see it. No. He can feel it move. Between his shoulder blades. Working through the blood and muscle. It opens and closes. Opens and closes. Its knuckles crack. Like a fire waking. Like a fire spreading. Gnawing limbs into night.

Wingspan

We decided it was time.
After three years in North Carolina,
we booked a cottage
dubbed "The Bird's Nest"
in a little mountain town outside Asheville.
We'd gone to the Biltmore.
A brewery with a putt-putt course.
Strolled downtown shops.
Had dinner at a local pizza haunt.
Then on the last night, our daughter, sprawled
in the Bird's Nest's
only bed, plate of leftover pizza
balanced on her lap, asked the number of days
she's been alive. Like a good
21st century father, I used Google
to calculate the days
from birth to Bird's Nest.
And there nested in the newsfeed, where, let's
face it, tragedy lives
beyond itself, I read a headline
celebrating a father's use of Google
to save his child's life
when a heart attack nearly killed him.
When *his heart broke*
the article says before it spills into confessing
the subsequent promise of love
whispered nightly
that provided the child the chance to tell
his parents who he really is—
a gay West African teen marching
unseen to a pulpit more than a decade of days.
Driving home to Greensboro
mist is religion. It spans
the mountains—an obfuscation of angels

holding hands wing to wing.
There's a heart inside it.
A kind of breaking. A certain awful aching
to be seen. Like the moment
a child asks how long
they've been alive. Our daughter
has been alive 2,818 days—one more
than this time yesterday.

Missing Headline

if it is missing it must be said it must be read in a headline I searched for a headline I couldn't find it must be bled through the sheets ghosts are made of it is the mud memory is made from it is delivered to the world by orphanage by distance by train by disconnection by track by brick by the sun winking dumbly against the coarse crystalline edge of a brick just before bloodied and just as dumbly against every blade of grass it finds itself lost within dropped without a thought or a dream it is a headline like little rock woman murdered like seven kids left behind it is mother murdered father in prison seven kids left behind it is seven kids to be sent to southern christian children's home it is after young mother murdered seven kids sent to orphanage it is seven kids left behind after mother murdered father in prison it is man kills sister-in-law with a brick kids sent to orphanage their father the murderer's brother in prison it is kids falling deeper into the dark places the maps don't show the places not found in the legend until they grow those places themselves until they shape the symbols they need to find their way out of them or inside them to curl up beside them to know how difficult it can be to grow up to grow inside this to grow away from this it is growing anyway it is laughing anyway and loving and having their own kids anyway new ghosts new memories new mud new bloodied sheets new bricks it is old and new bricks mortared together it is the brick any brick that brick my father always bit down on would have somewhere inside his mouth when he said anything at all this coffee is cold brick you have to try harder brick I'll pull this car over brick I have a voice like elvis brick don't you think brick when I sing brick I'm moving out for a bit brick not long brick a month or two brick maybe brick I have to go brick back to the county line brick for more booze brick show me your karate moves brick come on fight back brick come on fight brick I'm sorry brick I wasn't there when you were a kid brick I'm sorry I left brick I'm proud of you brick you know brick we all went to that shithole brick that hellhole brick I'm sorry brick I'm sorry brick my family is fucked up brick I'm sorry brick I'm brick I'm brick

brick

the fire that forms it requires stages
of division

(like anything
a few refusals
must be made—

       elements

     taken—

before the bestowal
of any gift)

Sprawling front lawn. Hill of broken toys. Dead December grass more gray than green against amber dark. Still every spear a story. Told or untold. 1,000 times or none. Larry exits one story. Enters another. The key finds its lock. Larry checks the knob. Larry breathes. Deep and deliberate. As if this breath is different than any other. Part of a plan. This the first sentence of breathing's last Act. One step. Another breath. For the last time, Larry leaves. He will take Highway 107 toward Morrilton. The next Act. Waiting in the wings.

Neither Sound nor Silence

My daughter wants to go on another joyride
with my father-in-law. To rattle down gravel paths
where island birds nip salty puddles—
feel the jitter of the exhausted golf cart they easily evade.
To go *out on a scud*, natives say. Or so I've read
in the blue pamphlet of Ocracoke brogue
bought for two bucks at the little museum by the pier.

But my daughter doesn't say *scud* or *joyride*.
Parked beside the screened-in porch
in its patch of rented grass, she just eyes the golf cart.
She hides anticipation to sweeten the ride.

By now she's learning to harbor a silence
peculiar to humans. I see in her brow the furrowed ghost
of my boyhood. On trips to Uncle Alan's farm
in Michigan, the adults sat for hours
in the large yard beside the house, sipping lemonade
in lawn chairs. Every time Grandma lit
another cigarette my gaze would lock on the barn.

In the dark only closed doors speak of
the golf cart sat in the silence of that telling. Behind
the barn, untouched by the cast spell
of my eyes, the cherry orchard wilted; the apple orchard
fell to ruin like Uncle Alan's collapsed lung.
I'd brave a tug on Grandpa's sleeve, and he'd know
it was time to bring the trails beneath us.

At the edge of the orchards, we'd find the eagles
nested in a copse of elms flanking acres
of open pasture. For hours we'd sit in silence, waiting
to see wings—hear the hush of our waiting.

Now, on the island, mourning doves are cooing
between seconds of silence. My father-in-law compares
the sound to counting time in a storm—a secret
whispered between the boom and the flash.
His granddaughter laughs. Soon a somnolent salt-wind
will carry him from the porch into dreams
of older stories. First, he'll buckle her next to him.
The scud of years ahead and behind.
The quiet aching to hold her open hand in his.

Inside My Grandfather's Death
Something Like 1,000 Horses

On his deathbed—
that's where I met him. My father's
father. Buried beneath
a contrivance of wires and tubes.
That hospital smell
vaguely metallic. Blue, somehow.
For a seven-year-old boy
this bewilderment a fog of light
and gauze.

There's the blur of people
waiting to say something to Donnie.
Goodbye. The only apology
for a secret wound. Rain
of promises. 1,000 horses leaping
a last time
over whatever fires behind their eyes
had never been
furnaced into words.

I learned later he was in the navy.
Went AWOL
when he felt an unbearable urgency
tug his collar toward the bar.
I learned
he beat his wife. Drove a diesel
if he could keep work. That he had
a distinct laugh. I learned
he drank himself into diabetes then
into the bed
I met him in, shriveling in every eye.
I learned he lived 52 years.

Before he died, we waited in a line
snaking down the bright hall.
He might've smiled
when my father finally stood me
beside his bed, said
take his hand.
My father—maybe he reminded him
my name. Maybe he said it
for the first time. The dying man
shivering to hear.
Me shivering to speak.

That night Uncle Wayne
held a small wake at his trailer.
Donnie's sons.
One brother. Me in tow.
They sat me on a faux tiger-skin rug
in front of the TV.
Maximum Overdrive
played on USA Up All Night
while they played music
in a back bedroom I never saw.

The next day my father wrote
a hot check—$1,000
for Donnie's coffin & burial service
to Apple Hill Cemetery.
I'd compare this to 1,000 horses
leaping inside him.
Inside his siblings. But I've learned
how we obscure ourselves
in our wounds.

After the wake, my father
kept the recording of their attempts
at a song for Donnie. It caught

a howl no one heard
when they broke for more beer.
Just before Wayne swears
something threw him against a wall.
I remember his voice
ballooning over the movie.

We played that tape for years
until it was lost
moving from the house on Fairview
to a rundown cottage
in the woods, where we were robbed
by one of Donnie's brothers.

Whatever rush of horses
we suffered then
is a story I can't tell. Instead, I try
to recall a distinct laugh
I never heard.

Time and Place (Unhorsed)

Most of the kids were home when it happened.

All except my father and one uncle—

>   the oldest two tasked to help
>   again on their grandfather's
>   modest farm.

Chancellor—the grandfather
on their mother's side—
exists only as a name for me.
>   A constellation
>   shipwrecked in a memory
>   the sky
>   can only vaguely shape.

I imagine most of my father's siblings—
the young ones at home who hid under the bed
as their mother was struck a final time—
still struggle to recover how that horizon
met those fields.

It doesn't matter what colors of green and gold
>   they saw unfold there—
>   fold
and unfold.
>   What shut their eyes
>   when a red fog
>   betrayed the body
>   that made them
>   no memory can unhorse.

>   Even for my father after eleven years
>   helping the horizon meet the fields
>   became
>   a time before.

Not long after
my father would know
                                another farm—
the Gordon family that fostered him.

            That sucker-punch of cow dung.
            His first dog a German shepherd pup.
            Learning to drive on an old red tractor.

So many bales of hay
he could climb to the bats in the barn—asleep
in the rafters—stacked against
the story
            that followed him there.

And
depending on the day
                        and where he found himself
standing in it
                        corn stalks tall enough
            (when he was unafraid to look)
            to fall
curling over the sun like
uncut hair.

Or at night   mantling the moon

                                the remains
of dead stars
            barely visible against the glow.

Back home—in the time before—
he wasn't there
                        when the brick vanished
                        from the window it held up.
                        He wasn't hiding
                        under the bed as if at play

when the hand that took it
                        warmed the carpet
                            with blood.
He wasn't there
and neither was I.
.
It doesn't matter.

                                    Later

on the Gordon farm—a name
    I'd know well—a name
                        not to hide from:

        a black Morgan horse named Bravo
        he would one day teach me to ride.

Under the Sun

If a person is murdered a person is murdered
most often by a person the person knows.
That's what the experts say.
The experts can't be wrong, right? Meanwhile
the sun says nothing—a white dot lobbed
over any city. Meanwhile a prison
is any city's darkest flower. Meanwhile any
ex-lover paroled can become a person
murdered or a murderer. Take the corner store
clerk in kakis. Who never spoke
or smiled. Who watched or who didn't watch
others enough. The cameraman. Your
optometrist. A drunk father.
The lifeguard at the community pool.
An acquaintance staying too late at the party.
You get the idea. Here, try this:
So, two bricklayers walk into a bar—stop me
if you've heard this one—one a murderer
one not. I don't know where
the joke goes from here, because I don't know
any jokes about murder. I wish I knew how
to say all of this without sounding
so phony. What's the thing people say—
you can't make this shit up. Okay
here it is then. My grandmother was murdered
by her brother-in-law. She knew him
as a father of six. Bricklayer. Her husband's
odd brother who rarely spoke—never
smiled. How could she know
he was a lover of a secret guilt, that
he often sat alone outside her house gripping
with gloved hands the wheel of
his '67 station wagon. Let me begin this way:
Larry was his name. 1970 was coming to

an end. He was pissed-off at
his brother, back in prison for beating his wife
and nearly killing another drunk at the bar.
Why wouldn't his sister-in-law
leave him? Larry listened to his thoughts.
They took him to the corner store
for a bottle. They took him inside a night that
swallowed the sun. They've
found me here decades later, saying
nothing about what followed my family after.

Ulteriority

[...] there are many other things I have found myself saying about poetry, but the chiefest of these is that it is metaphor, saying one thing and meaning another, saying one thing in terms of another, the pleasure of ulteriority.

—Robert Frost

How to say this? I'm caked in the filth of my father's secrets. When I say caked, I mean dreaming. When I say filth, I mean dirt. When I say secrets, I mean wounds. Yes. I am dreaming in the dirt of my father's wounds. When I say dreaming, I mean dreaming. I mean the night is long. I mean this bed a blade. When I say dirt, I mean a funeral. I mean the kind piled on. When I say wounds, I mean his mother murdered. Yes. I am dreaming. When I say dreaming, I mean waking. I mean held down by hands. When I say the night is long, I mean generations. I mean the trauma of time hunching at the foot of the bed. When I say this bed is a blade, I mean anything that aches away from its edge. When I say a funeral, I mean death will demand a ceremony. When I say piled on, I mean death will demand a ceremony. I mean grief. I mean the way grief beckons a breathing body. I mean hands. I mean a mouth. When I say his mother murdered there is nothing else to say.

brick

for the soft mud to become stiff—
harden into rock—
the heat must be increased
up to 1800 ºF
       the clay
          dehydrated
       any unused water
          purged

                (like anything—
                maybe nothing is closer
                to the truth
                for any human who any
                day may hold any

                    brick—

                a need must be created)

Pink neon disarranges fate. As far as Larry can see. In stars. In himself. Through the windshield of his station wagon. Larry sees. Stops for a box of Parliaments. A dark bottle. Its liquor the color of a viscous river. As if lifted from its palm. The same drink given to the trees. Here the dogwoods. There the pines. The living things among them still. The dead things among them more of the same.

Storm at The Drury Inn

We usually assume fireworks—
the sound of the sky
erupting above our neighborhood
like uncertain applause.
The coliseum less than a mile downtown,
we've stopped bothering
to part the curtains or raise the blinds.
Gunshots and storms
are why we left New Orleans.
In North Carolina we have a minor league
baseball team. Fair-weather
fandom. Enough pollen to write a sonnet
on the back windshield of our Subaru.
If our living room windows rattle,
it must mean a Grasshoppers victory.
Behind glass we're safe
to lose all the small battles we need to lose.
But tonight, four hours from home
five years now, which
somehow still seems new, we're at a hotel
in Knoxville. We're on our way
to unfavorable skies. My brother needs
help to quiet the voice
in his head. My father-in-law a new liver.
Though no ovations are coming,
we're waiting in the wings. But I have that
odd human feeling hotels
always conjure—how much
like home they can seem when I'm with
those closest to the lonely rooms
where I keep my love.
I applaud the night noises as they come.
Tonight, it's just plain old thunder.
Our daughter rushes
to the rattling windows to see.

Making a Sound

Bertolt Brecht said when the woods
                              are filled with police
you cannot write poems
                    about the trees.

When has our wilderness—
once human

                    once named—

          not been lit
          by blue light the opposite of dawn?

When have the songs of birds
              not been neglected
              by the noise
              of sirens
              clicked to the wind?

There is winter in the woods before
                              a dead body is hidden
under dead leaves.
              Winter then
              and winter after.
              We are allowed a moment

for making a sound
          when a bird misses a branch.
                              And when it lands.

brick

once all the water is gone oxidation
occurs
as the heat descends to 1,000 ºF
a little breath is blown
            into the brick

                    (like anything
                    we know before we know
                    —before we're told—
                    oxygen is a gift

                    if not from god's

                    mirrored mouth from all
                        the beauty and terror
                                it reflects:

                    the bloom of a flower and
                    the trauma of its slant
                    toward absence)

It's mid-December cold. Larry yawns. His gaping mouth a hole where night widens. As if inside the night another night. Larry pays no attention. Shuffles back to station wagon. Cranks the heat. Between chapped lips a cigarette. Before flame and smoke the shape of his breath—knot of snakes unkinked.

Respite

Under forgiving sun
in the backyard the dead
poison ivy snaking up the elms
is yawning back to life.
Two houses down
someone's mouth is pressed
to a trumpet. A few notes
blown among the birds.
Summers's last crickets. A dog
pawing a fence. That ghost-
noise of unseen cars.
I'm nursing a hangover with ice
in the coffee my wife
didn't drink before we left
on our hike down neighborhood
trails with the friends
we're visiting in Richmond.
I take a sip and imagine myself
as the baby snake
we saw before the last path
returned us to pavement.
I, too, just want to get across—
yawn my small yawn.

Education

If stuck in his mouth bricks bloody at the edges in the commissure of his lips my father will learn to spit bricks. They will fall fully formed at the end of every sentence to punctuate entire blocks for any to step over or trip. If rivers of grief sing choruses of bricks at his feet my father will learn to haunt like rivers. He will glide slightly drunk down neighborhood streets dimly lit like dreams of rivers. If asked to pause to pray at every sleeping window to say his song in slurs he will learn the night is made of children. Their smiles. Their crooked teeth. Fear and joy hiding in the hair draped over pillows. If my father questions the dead star's memory of his childhood bed he'll learn to be gentle. To be as silent as a brick on a windowsill in an empty room. A brick is innocent before it is used. If a brick was never used by his uncle to murder his mother my father could have learned what it means to not drink like a river. To not disappear like a bad dream that comes back to haunt the sleeping children with a mouth full of slurs that block out the sun brick by brick by brick by brick.

The House Where It Happened

It's cinematic—the house I have in mind.
No romantic landscape. Not a home
a painter might see from a distance passing it up
the tenth time in provincial rain
before shouldering the car to get a pic
of its loneliness lit by sliver of sun.

That house the painter's eye knows
the next drive will be gone—demolished
in a day. Somehow this is known.

What I see unfolds with a smell. Wild onions
leaning where the lawn hems
the sidewalk. Flank of edible flower clusters
fainting since the moment of birth.

My view is from the street they tilt toward
angling for me to come closer.
But I'm not really there. And I have never been.
Beyond the onions I see anyway
the grass needs mowing. Toys taken inside
or piled on the porch
before rain slants another sky.

I wanted the house to be any easily imagined.
A quick search on Google Maps.

I wanted a picture of the first day of spring.
A cheap painting reproduced on a For Sale sign
still standing after a new family
has settled in enough to worry about things
like the lawn. Too many toys
left out in too much rain. Wild onions.

Not how to say *before the murder*—not to know
what it means to say *after*. I wanted
a house haunted only by the normal things.

It must exist after the murder—let me start over.
Let me just say I've always enjoyed
that people often refer to levels of homes
as stories rather than floors.

Because floors are for dust. Spilled blood.
Lifeless things thrown in corners.
For measurements marking where one ends.

Where the next begins
story sounds better than *floor*.

The family after the murder—the house
empty of victims—they deserve
their own story. *The home
has only one story*—that's a good enough place
to begin. To inch toward another end.

And inside, people who sit sometimes on carpet
rather than chairs if struck
by a mood. Maybe to pet an aging dog.
Trace a finger back and forth
to invite the cat to do its acrobatics
for visiting relatives.

These are people who bathe babies
in sinks. People who grieve deaths of people.
People who make plans. College for their kids.
A trip out west. The right wedding gift.

People who step into the hall bathroom
then into the tub—a hand
flat against a robin egg wall—the other

lifting the window for it to fall
at the first turn away. Now on their way to find
something heavy to prop it up.
Unconcerned if whatever it is will one day
be used as a weapon, the family
fights over forgotten bills. Fresh carton of eggs
dropped. All of them broken.

I could do this all day. Describe every kid
listening behind closed doors
to music they aren't allowed to love.

Now a father who says *Listen to that bird*
whistling. It sounds so strange.
So close. Like it's inside. Like it wants
me to say how strange it is.

I wanted to begin this with a close-up
of a lawn. An unlocked door. The innocent
neighborhood noises surrounding
an imagined family. No mention of a mother
murdered. Not what sent the *before*
into *after*. Not what it did
to the kids—to their kids and to theirs.

Somehow, I've entered the picture. Slipped in
when the family wasn't looking.

There I am sprawled whistling on the lawn.
It's the first day of spring.
I sip coffee from my favorite cup.
Unconcerned with the smell of wild onions
like I too am something beautiful.

Like something that tells the imagined mother
to tell her kids *No, just a strange man*

lounging on our lawn
when what she really means to say is
every story is a ghost story.

Housepainter

Often, I conjure him.
It's easy—alone in the garage
slunk in a decaying
lawn chair with a cold beer
and the ghost,
trying to forget the house
he'd finished painting
an hour before.
Easy because he's painted
so many. Because
mornings begin with buckets
dragged to his van.
With drop-cloths cleaned and
re-rolled. With
joints aching beneath
speckled pants.
Because that rotten egg smell
of paint thinner stays
in the nose.
Because I've helped haul
the ladder—leaned it
against strangers' walls.
I've climbed with roller and
adjustable pole.
Because at home I'd hunch
beside him—wash
brushes under the spigot until
grass was milk.
Blue milk. Yellow milk.
Violet. Gray.
Every blade every color
of dying light.
Because he's downed
countless beers in the dark

of after. Because
from a house many houses
before he painted any
the buzz of a battery-powered
radio and a ghost
motherly beside him.
But it's never easy to enter
this darkness—wade in
for a story sealed like primer
beneath decades
of paint. Inside what
he dreams away from I need
pickaxe, shovel—
a language of digging up.
Something like blood
when I splay apart his past
like a hunted animal
with forgotten years clinging
to its fur and the fire
of pointed teeth
still gnashing to continue to
go on forgetting.
Something like a brick
in his chest—you can see it
glow through the skin
sometimes
under the light of the moon
if he's spent
the day—every difficult hour
alone with the truth.
This when he's nodded off.
This a silence
brightly lit. This shimmering
too familial to belong
(he must know)
to him alone. This a shape

untranslatable.
An unpaintable house.
Now to say his name
is to drop
a feather from the rooftop
of longing. Watch it
fall with the rain.
Watch the milky paint below
rise until it's lost in a sea
of feathers.
With seafoam eyes dreaming
toward the shore
I wish my father believed
it's natural to feel
lonely here—the past always
at dusk—where paint
will never dry before rain
marries the dark.

A Traditional Story of Exaggerated Consumption

For decades my father ate bricks for breakfast. It was hard to watch. The process obscene. This was no magician's trick. This a necessity. This a job. This was the most important meal of the day. Waking meant having dreamed. Having dreamed meant fever. Meant sweat. Meant the memory of his mother murdered with a brick. The memory of his mother murdered with a brick meant stumbling down the hall from that dream into morning. Morning meant the brick waiting for him on the kitchen table. Like a misplaced toy. Like a hat in a horror movie. Like that and like the alloy of absence. Like irony. In the beginning he built miniature houses. In every corner of our house another house. It was hard to learn to live among the clutter. He had to eat the bricks for breakfast, he decided. We had to go on living. He acted as if he knew it would always come to this. Every morning a brick for breakfast. Soon he could read the morning paper without gagging. His oatmeal left untouched beside him, he'd scrape the brick down. Sometimes he took the brick with him if running late. Maybe to meet co-workers at McDonald's before a new construction job. His Egg McMuffin waiting in front of him. Like a sob. Like a difficult question. Like an unwrapped gift. Sitting there beside the brick. Eventually he split town for good. Decided to stop eating the bricks. One drunken night a decade before, he told of a city inside him. A city that loved the bricks. That lived for them. That held grand ceremonies and sang songs as they arrived. A city that was nothing without him. Now, wherever he is, the bricks keep piling around him. A city that grief builds. Now, wherever he is, I search for any sign of him. I have my flashlight. My provisions. His name lodged like a brick in my throat.

brick

for vitrification to occur—the fire
intensified to 2400 °F—
the valence must be increased
this is when
the brick shrinks   when it becomes
something transformed:
a solid
impermeable
to water

           (like anything
           as the fire's delirium

                    swells

           the breath

           the brick was given—
           a gift that belies its
           mass—

           will be forgotten)

Larry drives. Drunk for maybe the second time in his life. The dogwoods—the pines—the world moves around him. Scrolls across the passenger window. Wild trains down hidden tracks. The pint of whiskey. A parasite. Mouths its closed-lip drone. Like a thought Larry has attempted to drown. Like whatever throbs. The station wagon slips a flat stretch of Highway 107. As if straight down an icy hill lit with dying light.

Driving in the Rain

Fun fact: during a thunderstorm
more raindrops fall than there are people
in the world. You can look it up.
I'll wait. Go ahead. But I won't bother.
My eight-year-old daughter—
everything she says deserves to be believed.
Besides, I'm driving. It's all true
anyway. Oz is over the rainbow. Just listen
to the tautology of water. Just look
at the summertime street—how it stretches
its torrid tongue beneath us.
A ghostly heat up ahead flails infinite arms.
We watch the rain fall, offering
platitudes in torrents. She says Blue Bird
(our Prius) can handle it. I know
the small human in back who says it
can handle it. The way she takes in the sky
over Benjamin Parkway—I'd
call it a bruise and be done with it. She uses
the opportunity to remind me
girls see more shades of color than boys.
Now she insists it's her favorite
shade of purple. This sky the same she used
for a surreal sketch of her mama's face
before we left the house. Now
she dangles a bracelet made with a friend—
late birthday present. The purple
meretricious gems. The fake feather barely
hanging on even with the windows up.
And just like that, she grows
taciturn, silent as the drenched blur of trees
scrolling by. I try not to, but I wonder
if she sees in her reflection
a semblance of how fractured we all end up.

How momentarily whole. How we
spread ourselves thin as we go. Raindrops
down a windowpane in a movie
about grief, we're reshaped—smudged over.
Each of us a palimpsest with a pulse.
At the risk of sentiment, I'll say nothing
is meretricious. Nothing fake.
It's all true. Inside every face a palatial sky.
Go ahead. You can look it up.
I'll wait beneath the rain of platitudes.

Artie Mae's Traveling Portrait

Through the night I've muddied my hands
to shape her image. The clay beside me a heap of red.
The fire to forge it a river of blue flame.

What can I hope to gain from this—telling these lies?
Manufacturing the heap. Feigning fire. Pretending I know
what I need to see to create. If I lift a likeness

of her it's from memories of a painting. The one that passed
between seven siblings every Christmas:
oil, applied thick; loose canvas; splintering frame.

When I was a kid, my father's year to keep the painting
circled around again, he'd lean it against the mirror
on the small armoire in his bedroom—curved cherrywood

framing carved flowers—to see himself beside her.
Before he slept. When he woke. To remember the whole dream
of her every night, his mother a flame that needed

no imagination. Not a body muddied by a river or a brick
bloodied by the hand that left it there. Not what I've written
down too many times. For now, I'd be content

with the curl of her smile when one of her seven children
stole a cigarette—hid in the bathroom *to be big.*
Or the cast of her voice when once, my father said,

she wailed to all of them: *you're driving me straight to crazy.*
When my father, the mama's boy he's said to have been,
had to ask, *can I go with you?* An image or two

is all I hope to inherit from her absence. From my father's.
I know I can't pry the brick from his mouth.
In stories I sneak myself into and out of—half-told

half-heard—I know only that I need to try.

Fog of Tongues

Once upon a time
                 words were beasts.
They stalked the things they named
until they became those things.
                 Fog
                  stumbled behind.

We lived and died in the direction of words—
a religion of everything unsaid.
             Not an image named.
Only sun and shadow—
that violent blur
               between
moon waxing gibbous   moon waning crescent.

Growing up I flung myself
toward the words
that fell slurring from my father's mouth—
                fished them
from the darkest slits
of our secondhand couch like lost coins.
             I flung myself
       toward and around and onto and inside.

His words were beasts—
       claws and teeth   dripping fur
      scared and shaking   so desperate

to cling to any expression suitable to name his misery
an ancestral strain mapped out in his blood.

Something like God   or something like
the thing without the word
for the thing.

Maybe a single moment that had never been
lit at the edges by his past—curled up by that violence
                    of words
                                is what he craved—
is what he tried to carve out of me.

Not the familiar strangeness of memory. Not
the mud it's made from.

Not always his absent father. Not so often in jail.
Not
the streaked glass where the brick propped open
the window
                        before it attempted to name
                                    all things.
One brick
the moment of its fall a mist
                            over everything after
that can ever be said—red brume—the blood
the uncle toed into the carpet like a bored boy

                    before he said the words
                your mother is going to be fine

before he hauled her dying where pines hem the river
            always midsentence
            just off highway 107.

If my father could wage such a war with words—
if he could stalk them circle them move toward
                and around and onto and inside—

if he could lose
                    I can whisper whatever prayer
                                this is.

brick

the brick achieves its color
from the minerals in the fired clay—
raw materials taken
from the surrounding environment
where the brick is manufactured

                              (like anything
                              the brick doesn't know
                              where it came from—

                                   what shovel

                              when clay
                              was awakened
                              from its ancient dream—

                              whose gloved hand

                                        this fire)

The station wagon scuds to a stop. As if the man driving doesn't know how he arrived. The gravel driveway coughs red dust. Larry becomes one ungloved hand. Lifts itself from the wheel. Finishes the whiskey. Allows the bottle to fall. Wonders if the color of night is not black or blue but dark red.

Summer Reading

Barely noon and already the heat
has a mouth. A taste for the creative
blabbering of fanatic augers
scanning ancient skies for sick birds.
I should really be teaching
my daughter to swim, the dissipating
clouds seem to say in amorphous
sentences written across
my bare, sunscreen-lathered chest.
But here comes Rebecca, newly
engaged and glowing,
her gift for my daughter's birthday
in tow. She's ready to jump in,
raving over a new docuseries
about the professional mermaid biz.
Fun pool-worthy topic, to be
sure. But I can't listen to her. Even
when she delivers the line
from the glum mermaid in Arkansas:
"You know, it's really hard to be
a landlocked mermaid."
I'm an ok humanitarian. I'm reading
Hass instead of the sky. But
none of us are doing the best we can.
I pretend to read the green
hardback pointed to the sky but I'm
conjuring a comparison.
The first cold shock of early summer
freshly chlorinated water begs
a poolside metaphor, doesn't it?
Maybe something about the war and
the other war or the other war
compared to lonely floaties
deflating in the deep end. Or maybe

time's carnage of goodwill
to towels drying on plastic chairs.
Yes, the sky sends its fire down.
Yes, it's time again to be by the pool.
For this, too, I am unprepared.

My Father's Grief

If in the forest it grew it could carve a door. Could build a bridge to cross the river. Could forget its haunt of snakes. If any eldritch shape could uncoil. If it could fashion a field beyond it. If in that field a dance of wind in the grass. If it could romance the sun. Could harness the stars. A single light an ethereal moment to light the way. If lambent in any season. If at the edge of distant skies. If a hill blue with distance with water with reflection. He might find a tumulus to mourn beside. Because his frayed brush is no talisman. Because he cannot bristle this into existence. Because no coat applied to this house. Because the one before. Because the next—he drags his bucket of black paint through the dark garage. Because this his only paroxysm. Because time and its dead. Because crawling into corners. Because decades of cobwebs. Because memory means frosted breath. Means dust sculptures. Means pills for hills. Means every moment a mote. Decades made of days made of dust. Because my father. Because he shuffles through this. Because again he drags his bucket of black paint through the dark garage. Through the splashing sound in his wake. Through the scraping of speckled boots. Because this dance. Because every dusk. Because no other color exists. Because the bucket. Because what's inside. Because what he leaves behind. Because it blackens the grass. Because he turns the faucet until it spits. Because it rinses the paint from the brushes but can't clean his hands.

brick

regardless of natural color
clay containing iron in any form
will exhibit a shade of red when
exposed to an oxidizing fire

(like anything
a brick will always appear

red
when spattered with blood)

An accomplice—still running—the station wagon waits. The ungloved hand makes its exit. Drags with it the man it belongs to. Stands in the yard. Grows eyes. Gawks. Flicks cigarette into birdbath. Hears it hiss. Reaches to tie right boot. And though no one will be able to testify, sees everything it sees with red eyes. Windblown yard. His brother's car left behind. The elms beyond the house. Towering above it. The people inside. Real and imagined. Living in its lit corners. And somewhere inside Larry another ungloved hand. Somewhere a thought. A flattened palm. Fingers curling up. As if to mimic claws. Miming the grip of an object. Testing the weight of it. And absence the only revelation. That the absence of any brick will always weigh the same as the absence of anything.

Minor League

He's gorgeous, his brother—looks like Jared Leto.

In front of us the Grasshoppers
making quick work of the Asheville Tourists.
A row behind, Stacy's friend Shannon—
hotdog in hand, oversized beer between the knees—
hungry for more about my brother.

Before Stacy relayed his relative beauty
she'd shifted around to find her friend's eyes.
She'd said it with such gusto,
such promise to beguile—I thought I'd drop it.

By the time the conversation landed
on his looks, I'd already rattled off, compiled since
prepubescence, his bouts with bad luck
easily remembered—easily said.
Josh, my brother, seven years younger, Jared Leto
lookalike, cell tower climber:

Bitten by brown recluse. Stung by 14 wasps
at once. Head bludgeoned by corner
baseboard. Kid on four-wheeler hit by truck. Fallen
angel at bottom of playground
slide. Face struck by Braves game pop-foul.

What harm would it do to stop there—leave them
to imagine a fetching specter
strolling through their innocuous afternoon.

A Saturday of scheduled fireworks. Tiered seating
bathed in sun. The only embarrassment
a pit stain or two. The harmless recurrent boom
of a t-shirt cannon. The flinch after.

What good would come from inviting them
to see him hanging from the rafters
in our mother's garage—hear the metal trestle give
under his weight. To see him hiding
in strangers' cars—hear the voices he hides from.

I don't tell them he's removed the knob
from every door in his house. That no closed space
is safe unless he can see out.
Best to leave his suffering in the minor league.
A handsome phantom selling hotdogs.

Ghost-man on first gone astray midfield, searching
for the medication he can't remember
tossing over the chain-link fence.
Like us all, a specter among spectators.

He's really gorgeous—more like Jake Gyllenhaal.

Elvis Impersonator

Only in the car, only leaving or arriving,
my father sang like Elvis.
Any stretch of road longer than a song
the ghosts swarmed the streetlights. Trauma
tangled nests in the trees. Every corner
a corner where his fear and shame
huddled like orphan siblings around barrel fires
no one saw. First, in the rearview
I saw his green eyes drift toward mine
as he backed out of our gravel driveway; beyond
the windshield's cracked glass
a blue house growing smaller on its hill.
The radio already on, after a few practiced flicks
of the knob, he'd lift a scrap—
whatever slapdash pop hit suited him.
No matter what it was, he turned it into Elvis.
Because my mother loved Elvis.
I knew nothing haunted that house.
Its path of loose gravel coughing dust. Deep blue
like a voice finding the King's baritone.
Alone like eyes in a mirror of trees.
I knew it like I knew his palm would lift
from the wheel. The sound of the slapped dash
a gesture designed for his wife
to lend an ear. Me in the back, searching
the rearview. There's my baby brother beside me.
Plump. His breath bubbling spit.
The radio is cranked, the old man leaning in.
Springsteen's "Pink Cadillac."
Somebody tempting somebody. And just like that
his silence like a house on fire.
Decades later, I'm driving to get my mother
from the airport. My daughter asked
to ride along. The windows down, we blast

Lady Gaga. Soon enough I'm singing, slowing
every word of "Poker Face"
to a blue baritone. Behind princess sunglasses,
somewhere adrift in the rearview,
my daughter's eyes searching for mine.

brick

to give it another color
a brick may be flashed
in the fire   its interior will retain
the tone of its first flame
the heart
its original blush

        (like anything
        it's difficult to discern
        whether or not the murder

           any brick

        may help happen
        achieves its color
        the way a shovel achieves
        in the moment
        of the first downward

           thrust

        the color of clay)

Close by. Somewhere someone has flung the night open with one door. Now. Here. The screen slaps the wall on the wrong side. Kisses the brick. The house turns to hear. As if it had forgotten to stand watch. As if to ask. What to be ready for? Now the heavy door. The wooden one. Now slowly. Now there. Rigid against the night. The outline of a man standing in the threshold. A statue that moves.

Family Movie Night

When Iceman appeared—that's when you got teary.
I know you know. I just need this moment
to say I saw you. That I knew before we pressed play
how it would all go down. You cozy on the couch
next to your dad. The window to your left
an idyllic display of Christmas snow. The dog asleep
by the patio door. The cat on her pillow.
I knew we'd settle into that cinematic image. The family
on movie night—enough popcorn to purge
our pity and fear. I sneaked a look at you between bites.
At the beginning of every scene: Maverick,
the wild pilot careening through clouds; Maverick
reprimanded; Maverick elbowing the bar.
Then it happened as if scripted, your flinch the moment
Maverick entered Iceman's office. There was Val
wearing a scarf to hide the hole in his gorgeous throat.
And somehow you were also there, hiding
somewhere under his massive desk—a scared kid
in a red baseball cap. The one I've been told
you wore for years. Your objective correlative
when you demanded your brothers call you Maverick.
Your keeper of dreams the best defense
against a blur of adult fears focusing into view.
What I'm trying to say is I saw you. Beneath the blanket
that belongs to the couch, cozied up by the old man.
Yes, but also kneeling at the grassy edge
of your childhood. Coaxed there by the fire of it
inside the cave of it inside the forest of it.
Because grief is where aging begins, you forced a laugh
when your dad said he named the pills
he refuses to take Vincent—the world rendered
a Van Gough painting. And because crawling
in the direction of that laugh meant crawling through
a forest dark as the future, you crawled

out of your skin to find yourself under a desk in a movie
about fighter pilots. You carried there the news
of your dad's diagnosis: the first cancer
cleared—now the spot found on his liver. *Time to let go,*
Iceman typed. Below the words someone sang.
You saw it in Maverick's eyes. The anaphora of grief
and what guides us through it: the window
to your left; the fire in the family room, waiting
to be resurrected; the screen's dusty eye
staring you down; the runtime; the closing credits.

Hunting for Haunted Houses

Finn asks if we can go. *Looking for haunteds*, she calls it.
I've had enough coffee to say yes. I've listened
to the right music, and the rain has promised to meet me
on the bridge to the past. I know. But really though
it's going to rain. Soon the clouds will begin
their strangeness of folding in half the distance between
memories and ghosts. I don't mention this.
Finn finds her new toy. Grabs her coat. Five minutes
and we're hunting. She enjoys these little drives.
We always take our aging pug. He rides
in the back with her. His tongue hanging out, fat and pink
like a baby eel. Finn likes knowing how to feel.
A *haunted* means a door is left open. It's as simple as
a cracked window. Peeling paint. Sometimes
you can tell a lawn wants a feral fog to snake through it.
Wants you to imagine it happen. Almost always
there's a second story—at least two. Obvious attic above.
The usual jaunt through usual neighborhoods,
none seem right. Here, too many cats curled in too many
tulips. There, the absence of cats and tulips.
Then she spots one—she knows. Three-story brick.
Attic window cracked. White lights strung over shutters
since last Christmas. Front door standing
slightly open. Dim inside like a lie you tell yourself
you never told. In the rearview, Finn's eyes
are all aflame. She's proud of her find. Then I start to feel
shitty about our little game. We know nothing
about ghosts that do or don't drift through walls hidden
beyond walls we can see. But neither of us
are ready for me to end this—tell her what's made me
stranger. She asks if the haunted has a basement.
Now she tells the dog that we don't have
a basement at home. I don't say every haunted
has a basement even if it doesn't. We hunt down another.

A Traditional Story of Exaggerated Conception

I've lived inside my father's past. A child in a small town. I've come to rest. I've gone in silence to the deserted square. My teeth bared to my own shadowless steps. I've studied the midnight flickering of lonely streetlights. I've rubbed my back against the beams. To dream of shedding. To sing my becoming. To skin myself against the ghost of hands that led me there. But I never entered the forest at the edge of town. If you're wondering, of course I haven't. Because I know a crown of wounds waits. See it happen? To brave the forest is to discover I was born there. In other words, do I have to say that I am afraid of everyone? Tell you that I am afraid of myself the most? Avoiding the fanged howl of the forest I stroll over crushed pianos on sleeping lawns. Every broken key. I shake the sleeping trees. Between the branches, sibilant whispers on my father's lips. Every syllable another crushed piano. His mother. Her murder. Louder now. His mother. Her murder. And again— her name. He says her name. Any tree at night knows her name by heart. Knows mine and knows his. Knows it like lights strung from a porch—their burning bulbs—are enough to know someone is home. My father is there somewhere. I am here somewhere. We are nowhere everywhere.

brick

for bricks made
from various raw materials there is
no direct relationship
                                between
strength and color   or absorption
and color

                              (like anything
                              all properties of a brick—
                              its raw material
                              a blended composition
                              of clay—
                              is an achievement
                              of desire:

                                    a manufacturing process
                              nothing other than

                                    flame's manipulation)

To change the shape of the world, a simple process. A door is left open. Here, night must be allowed an entrance. Larry leaves the door open. Night follows behind him. Moves toward and around and onto and inside him. Larry trails red dust. Boot prints stamped into carpet. White shag. He hasn't done it yet. Hasn't made it past the living room. Still the witnesses must begin immediately. The kids. Six of them. To imagine. Not the fire an empty hand holds. But somewhere in the distance glistening. Somewhere in the unmapped. Somewhere in the memory of other hands. The door to another dawn.

The Path of Totality

There was no sound. The eyes dried, the arteries
drained, the lungs hushed. There was no world.

—Annie Dillard, "Total Eclipse"

Every wall in our house is a spectacle.
That's what happens
when you're too tired to move.
And if you stand staring
long enough in any room you can hear
the walls of photos beg
to be weakened to whispers.

My wife, because it's still not real that
her father has died, searches
the walls—peels back the truth from
its little tricks and fictions.
I burrow into other news—
a world of suffering whittled down
to an email listserv.

Today something nonhuman: the total
solar eclipse is tomorrow.
Somehow, we'd missed the mania
in our fog of grief. Turns out
the path of totality crosses Carbondale
again—the college town
where Phil died in home hospice.

In 2017 the total solar eclipse brought
more than 14,000 visitors
to southern Illinois for the viewing.
In 2024, no one came to view
Phil's body because Phil
refused a funeral. He hated the event
and the spectacle—the idea.

I like the idea of humans holding hands
as they look up to witness
the event. I like knowing the things
they'll say—*daytime darkness,*
the path of totality—the umbraphiles
praying for cloudless skies,
knowing there's nothing to be done.

Image is to Word as Brick is to Murder

Brick. Finally, this morning, without thought
you jot down the word
on a used envelope. Quick scribble
over the place where the paper was torn—the fold flared
into pointed teeth. Harmless
as the offer inside to consolidate debt. Harmless as you
deciding the word itself is nothing
without the image beneath it. To push past impulse
without question is to invite
brick to become *murder weapon.* As it did—as it does
every time you sit down to write.
Now it's happened. Now you're thinking. Now you attempt
an unreadable scrawl. Deliberate. Like learning
to fall on purpose. *Murder weapon*—
closer to Wordsworth's *one human heart* of the image—
attached to the action of what happened.
Soon enough you move on
to *mother*—what the murder weapon erased
from your eleven-year-old father.
Now *ripped*—how he was taken from dreams designed
by rifts in dreams. By domestic abuse.
By poverty. By alcoholism. By family. Like anything rigid
against the absence of Wordsworth's rainbow,
what is possibly there
waiting for him to return home? Childhood a nightmare
of falling. Adulthood a long wake
for what fell. You return to your first impulse.
Jot it down again—*Brick.*
You wish your father's name was printed beneath it.
You wait for some sign of him to arrive.
In tomorrow's mail. The next. The evening news. The sky
on a cross-country drive going home. Now
you slip into the driver's seat. Pocket the envelope.
Your young daughter, strapped snug

in her cow-print booster,
takes the workbook you hand her—
matches shapes of words with pretty pictures.

Crueler than Fiction

Maybe the boy is an only child. Close with his father, every third Sunday
they skip church, pack the car for a trip to Pinnacle Mountain.
At the last precipice they enjoy a light lunch with the view. If it rains, God is
in the rain. Maybe the boy's mother crosses Rock Island Bridge
walking home. Broken road slick with rain, a cement truck loses control.
Flung over the edge, her body sinks like a brick into the river.

Maybe the boy loves walking with his sister to the farmers market a mile
into town. To school in the whisper of snow Arkansas winters.
The pond by the apiary on their grandparents' land. This is where they break
into a run. Sweat through the buzz the bees make. Like his pulse,
purpose lives in every step. Like a swarm, at home horrible voices alive
in the brick. Again, he's greeted. Again, his mother's disease.

Maybe the boy is the oldest of three. His mother a widow. A wiz at math
like her, the boy teaches his brothers to be practical. To count
on fingers—on hands. To multiply columns of time. Their world will always
work itself out to work against them. Be ready, the boy teaches.
When his mother dives into a well the boy gathers his brothers beside it.
To count until committed to memory the number of its bricks.

Maybe the boy's twin sister dies at birth. A brother born the next summer
lives two years before his heart outgrows the chest that holds it.
Something grows inside the boy. The life that death builds. Nightly he waits
by the window. He makes a wish—watches as it goes feathering
through the branches. Every tree his favorite tree. Any sapling a sibling.
His mother's stomach grows again. A tumor as big as a brick.

Maybe the boy is adopted. Maybe he grows up on a modest farm growing
corn for his adoptive parents, tending cattle. A small-town star
on the high school football team, he gets a full ride at University of Arkansas.
Going pro not in the cards, he decides to coach. Like God, the sun
follows him home. Like the moon, he never marries. Chooses to adopt.
His father calls with bad news. The phone a brick in his hand.

Maybe the boy isn't one of seven. Maybe his father, not an absentee father, is not an alcoholic. Doesn't abuse the boy's mother. Isn't often in jail. The boy's mother—her brother-in-law doesn't covet her affection, his car never parked down the street on quiet nights. The boy doesn't have to save her because his uncle never decides to break in. The boy's mother will not be murdered with a brick. Bricks do not exist.

brick

when subjected to rising
temperatures
clay or shale   unlike metal
melts gradually
                    softens slowly
final drying takes place
at temperatures up to about 400 ºF
temperatures will vary

                    (like anything

                        a brick

                    is measured against
                    its toughness its tone its

                        touch its

                    length and width)

In the bathroom. Ill-lit by flicker of dying bulb. Cold as its tile. Cold as a whole bottle of spilled pills. Cold as December's ghost misting the backyard. Edging inside through the window. Cold as Larry reaching for the brick that props it up. Reaching like a Stygian dream that chases the sleep of a silent guilt. That chases a motive to replace it. Reason enough. Murder for the woman that makes him live. Always this way. In a fog this dense. In this dim Cimmerian trench. This myth. Murder for the woman that will not listen. The woman that must love her husband's drunken abuse. His prison sentence and its end. Murder for her. A brick. The woman that will love his brother instead of him.

Traveling Home to Arkansas

Before long I end up standing alone
on the mole-tunneled lawn
beside my mother's house, staring
into the quiet pines flanking
a forest across the street.
I'm a character in a movie, lost
in contemplation. I'm waiting. I'm
listening with tilted head.
Because somewhere beyond
the needled branches the creature
making creature noises
will any second now reveal itself
once and for all. You've seen
enough movies to discern its nature.
You know it won't arrive.
No matter its tentacled shadow
or the crack of fallen limbs
beneath its prowling step. The heat
of its breath or the drumming
of its heart only I can hear
over the university library's bells.
No matter if I've arrived home
for a funeral or holiday or wedding
or because my brother
can't be left alone for more
than a day—the voices
that judge every decision he makes
unmasked and rampaging.
No matter if we've said a word
to our father in months or yesterday
he called finally to ask
for forgiveness. The creature
in the trees in the movie in the poem
is me. I know it always is.
Knowing the truth has never
kept me from waiting for it to arrive.

Missing Story

if it is missing it must be told it must be nearly christmas it must be dusk crouching in the windows like a dying animal it must be hiding behind darkening walls where poverty demands dinner plates licked clean where the kids can settle into place where quotidian actions of play can hatch domestic shadows there in the kitchen a toy car shivering across cold linoleum there a secondhand doll climbing into its bed of laundry there a cardboard crown a shield with crayoned coat of arms a plastic sword drawn to the vacant hall where none of them know how far patterns cast against tonight's walls that every night after will begin begging comparison compare their relative innocence to the drag of the brick against the window frame that throat-clearing rasp compare flecks of blue paint only the house hears fall to silence as a breath against glass compare seeing blue paint chips piled on the floor beneath the windowsill as feathers missing from a bewildered bird to none of them seeing the man sneaking out of the bathroom with a brick none of them hearing his human mouth expel a human breath compare the weight of passing decades to the weight of his breath lingering like a fog against the glass that it will remain a lingering fog to now down the hall the kids shadowing their mother's scream their eyes open narrow as dust to them becoming a part of something crueler than fiction something trapped in the storied darkness beneath the bed compare the demands of being trapped to drawing a map of the sky on the floor where dead bugs are fallen stars where seconds before stories kept the world what it was where now a monster claws out a story that never ends because it's never told where now the feet of their father's brother now the raised hand they can't see or the brick it holds or the brick it holds or the brick held in the falling silence compare this to christmas to every story the mother ever told crouching in the windows

brick

brick manufacturing
is among the most methodical
manipulations
of unshaped clay
to produce a product—to give
rise to

                a consequence

                                        (like anything a brick
                                        will become
                                        something bigger
                                        than itself:
                                        wall
                                        road
                                        murder weapon
                                        well
                                        doorstop
                                        fire pit
                                        window prop
                                        hell

               wall
               road
               murder weapon
               well
               doorstop
               fire pit
               window prop
               hell)

In the living room. Lit by children at play. Five on the floor. One in the crib. Clutching thin slats of wood. A mother folding laundry into a pile. A corner of toys. A cheap lamp leaning. Its shade. The wall that supports it. Not yet covered in blood. Now a man. Familiar. Now the thing the hand holds. Strange. The way it's raised. The way the mother doesn't see. Not the man. Not the familiar thing strange in his hand. Now like a dream. Like make-believe. Like the scene in a movie that scatters birds.

Here Comes the Rain

Between the sea and the salt marsh
my in-laws' bijou beach house squats on stilts
above a thicket of cordgrass
and bluestem, where for the last two nights
some critter, hidden from my phone's
dim flashlight in the brush below the back deck,
has made its noise toward the water.

It's Mother's Day. Sarah's mom sits
on the deck, reading while she reclines
in a plastic Adirondack; Sarah, silent beside her,
does the same—a book on women surrealists
held up awkwardly to block the sun.

The kid's couched, gripped by the unflinching eye
of an iPad, so I step out to ask the mothers
if they'd prefer that I go to the closest grocery
for cinnamon and vanilla—I'd promised
to cook French toast. *Appetite doesn't demand it,*
Sarah says. Her mother's nod agrees.

I point out a kettle of hawks sporting the blue
above a lone cormorant—the span
of its unfolded wings meant to intimidate
any predator. Sarah nudges past me,
grabs the binoculars that belong to the house.

When she's finished, she passes them to me
and returns to the tabled book. I fumble to adjust
the settings, scan the scar of land
jutting out from the marsh but can't spot
the cormorant. Instead, I find the American flag
at the edge of the neighbor's deck.

Last night, after everyone had gone to bed,
a strange shadow whipped
back and forth across the marsh. I didn't know
right away what the black swath
belonged to, but when I attached shadow
to flag, I wished I had the drugs needed
to help me see it—to face or forget whatever it
might've meant. I mention this to Sarah—
make my noise toward the kitchen.

At the oven I'm still holding the binoculars.
Dizzy from looking through their lenses
I stumble back to the deck, hand them over.
But before I head in, I notice the sky
blurring a bit, swearing an oath to rainclouds,
and remember that roar
we'd heard at the beach the last two days—
like the sky was shedding its skin.

This the kind of thing I would've discussed
with my father-in-law if he were here
rather than everywhere. As far
as my own father goes, he could be anywhere.
Could've heard the same sound.

We'd thought the roar had to be planes hidden
by clouds; or a rumble of thunder.
But there were no clouds at all. I thought
of what Kerouac said about the sea,
which I read on the little square of embroidery
above the toilet in the guest bathroom.
That it must be *the roar of eternity*.

I think now there must be a major insinuation
I'm missing—now, the moment
when the rain begins to come down.

The House After It Happened

If you looked through a window

        in the back bathroom
        you'd see—

gripped in its square
of cracked glass—

kudzu snake down
           distant elms.

There   skirting the edge of the creek
    just beyond the edge
          of the
          property.

Closer   an abandoned doghouse

withered under six summer skies
since the hound named and
       renamed died
         under one.

Once my father told me everything I love
deserves a name.

Here
   the nameless swing set—
      though there's no one willing
to push another into the sky—
      the kids still pretend with.

There
      an eleven-year-old
      form of my father
      brooding by the slide.

As if separate from the scene.
As if removed
                    from the window.

He looks lost in a song he doesn't sing.

His silence the shape of
                    all that has passed
            that might never find words.

                    Like a brick

that collapses
                    a window

when lifted like a secret from its sill

                    nothing is so silent

that it will not be heard.

From outside my father might one day
                        imagine—
the way a flicker of sun finds the vase
of cut flowers—
                    another interior.

Somewhere a house in a different dream.

                For now
if his mother murdered
with a brick—her brother-in-law
                who held it—

        is the song he is lost inside
he'll learn to hum along

like a window that sees
                    only
                    what it can see.

And look—
somehow there I am
                    holding his hand.

Hand-in-Hand

The children have broken free from the house. Its fictitious underworld. This myth. Its chthonic. This ersatz basement where they've waited. Stepped into ghosts wherever they stepped. Whenever they stepped in and out of their skins. Piles of them. Discarded in the corners. They've pantomimed this moment. Rehearsed it. Now they go glowing through the nighttime streets. This runaway cluster of stars. Confusing electric lights. Amazing the neighbors. Who part the curtains. Who pinch back the blinds. These the children that silenced time in the bricked darkness of that depth. They have dressed in that cold. Waked and slept in it and didn't dream. Now their glowing skin. Now made of their mother's memory. The flame of her breath in their hair. They sing into every puddle that catches a glimpse of them. They mimic the stillness of tangled trees. With their ancient laughter. With their crooked teeth. With the dirt of neglect painted across their cheeks in splotches. With a wave the branches part to let them pass. From any dying night to the pasture of sun just beyond it. Hand-in-hand they bright. They walk. They break into a run. Hand-in-hand. Into its muddy heart. They fall on their backs to angel the clay. Hand-in-hand. They cry out for all of us. Hand-in-hand. Gather into the sky.

brick

in the beginning
for a brick to become
           a solid mass
melting must occur

when the clay
breaks down
    becomes
         molten—
      a deformed shape—
the key is control
of the fire

          (like anything
          for a brick to become
           a murder weapon
          a process
          is replaced with
          a process—

                 a person

          with the object

                 a person
          holds)

Epigenetics

Evidence suggests telling the story
of trauma can create
new trauma—even if the trauma
or its story is not your own.

I have to wade into this poem.
Pants rolled past the knee. I have to be
a river valley's crooked silence
mistaken for sound.

To tell this story, I have to swim out
to the middle of the river
where the current rushes. I have to
love the carnage of its spell.

It's easy to imagine my father's past
as a broad swath of alluvium—
deposited from loss.
Something left behind. Something

made from clay. Something that fell
like silt through parted fingers
on a massive hand. The other hand
holding an unfolded map.

I'm in the river now. Waist deep.
I remind myself when the water carves
its memory into mud
the remaining rock often endures

fertile soil. I glance back to the bank
I came from. A child
that isn't there sifts the sand
that isn't there. For anything to keep.

It's said children carry everything
their parents have left
unattended. There are actions to take—
the experts say—tell the story.

We say *haunted* to qualify wild eyes.
And when we say our past
is coming back to haunt us our eyes
are unmapped islands.

Untold stories of ghosts stranded
on corners of old streets
with new names. They watch waiting
for words to lift their sheets.

What strange bird is perched there
to welcome me in? To what
underworld? Me with my living skin,
my pretend newspaper clippings—

stories of what sins say about blood
and what they don't.
My father's and mine, his father's
and his. A catalog of sharks

lost in a river. They're here with me.
I've carried them out.
I've gone chest deep. I've brought
decades of newspapers

folded into boats. Each gets a palm
of sediment. Each is dragged
back to the bank. There I shape them
into things without memory—

dead relatives and living—
with no mother's murder imprinted
on their genes. Still, they say
a river can never forget what is done.

I don't want my daughter to wade
the waters of this dream.
But if she submits to the river valley
of its crooked silence—

says goodbye in a language of clay
to a great-grandmother
she never met (the ghost of a woman
neither of us knew)—

I'll tell the story. Tell it delicately.

Acknowledgements

Grateful acknowledgment is given to the editors of journals in which versions of the following poems were first published (listed in the order of appearance in the manuscript):

"Prologue" published as "Missed Calls" in *Poetry*
"Wingspan" in *Rattle*
"Missing Headline" in *Fence*
"Neither Sound nor Silence" in *Unlikely Stories*
"Inside My Grandfather's Death Something Like 1,000 Horses" in *The Indianapolis Review*
"Time and Place (Unhorsed)" in *Pedestal Magazine*
"Under the Sun" in *Superstition Review*
"Ulteriority" in *Radar Poetry*
"Storm at the Drury Inn" in *North American Review*
"Making a Sound" in *Xavier Review*
"Respite" in *Raleigh Review*
"The House Where It Happened" in *Iron Horse Literary Review*
"Housepainter" in *Poetry Online*
"A Traditional Story of Exaggerated Consumption" in *Jet Fuel Review*
"Driving in the Rain" in *Rattle*
"Artie Mae's Traveling Portrait" in *Mudfish*
"Fog of Tongues" in *Pedestal Magazine*
"My Father's Grief" in *Harpy Hybrid Review*
"Minor League" in *New Orleans Review*
"Elvis Impersonator" in *Connecticut River Review*
"Hunting for Haunted Houses" in *The Poetry Buffet: An Anthology of New Orleans Poetry* (New Orleans Poetry Journal Press)
"A Traditional Story of Exaggerated Conception" in *Laurel Review*
"Image is to Word as Brick is to Murder" in *Pedestal Magazine*
"Crueler than Fiction" in *Pinch*
"Here Comes the Rain" in *The Comstock Review*
"The House After It Happened" in *Xavier Review*
"Hand-in-Hand" in *Eunoia Review*
"Epigenetics" in *Iron Horse Literary Review*

*The experimental pieces that begin with "brick" were published as "Brick" in *Denver Quarterly*

My deepest gratitude for the people near and far who have helped to shape me and my work over the years.

To my teachers Rodger Kamenetz, Laura Mullen, Andrei Codrescu, Mari Kornhauser, Rick Lott, and Jo Ann Steed, thank you for opening the right doors at the right time. Many thanks as well to all my teachers outside the classroom. You may not know who you are, but I do.

Deepest appreciation for my dear friends Vincent Cellucci, Brock Guthrie, and Lonnie Atkinson for your continued support. The love you have given my work is a constant light.

Thank you to the friends who kept my heart alive and well as I burrowed head-first into the mud of this project: Mark Beurhing, Kathy Goodkin, RJ Hooker, Susan Kirby-Smith, Josh Watson, Jen(n)ifer Tamayo, Sean Cain, Bill Lavender, Nancy Dixon, Brett Evans, Jonathan Penton, Roz Spencer, Adrian Van Young, Darcy Roake, Jordan Soyka, Veronica Barnes, Erik Beerbower, and Maura Way.

So much love to my family for accepting a poet in their midst (and for all that brand of acceptance means), especially my partner Sarah (Dagger) Jackson and our daughter Finn, without whom this book would not be possible—thank you, thank you, thank you! 1,000 times thank you!

This book would also not be possible without the devotion to the art of poetry from everyone at Brick Road Poetry Press. Thank you for trusting my work and giving it such a wonderful home. Miriam Calleja, Halley Cotton, and Matt Layne—you are all heroes!

A last thank you to Nick Cave and the Bad Seeds, whose albums *Skeleton Tree* and *Ghosteen* were near constants during the early stages of this book, and to the poets whose work I was devouring along the way: Brad Richard, Brandon Shimoda, Carolyn Hembree, Diane Seuss, Kerrin McCadden, Natalie Diaz, and Sara Henning.

www.ingramcontent.com/pod-product-compliance
Lightning Source LLC
Chambersburg PA
CBHW041719090426
42739CB00019B/3487